Heaven On Earth

My Vision of Yogaville

By H. H. Sri Swami Satchidananda

D1488204

Integral Yoga® Publications
Yogaville, Virginia

Heaven on Earth: My Vision of Yogaville
By H. H. Sri Swami Satchidananda

Publications by Sri Swami Satchidananda

Beyond Words

Enlightening Tales

The Golden Present

Guru and Disciple

The Healthy Vegetarian

Integral Yoga Hatha

Kailash Journal

The Living Gita

To Know Your Self

Yoga Sutras of Patanjali

Publications about Sri Swami Satchidananda

The Master's Touch

Sri Swami Satchidananda: Apostle of Peace

Sri Swami Satchidananda: Portrait of A Modern Sage

Boundless Giving: The Life and Service of Sri Swami Satchidananda

Satchidananda Ashram-Yogaville, Buckingham, Virginia 23921, USA

www.yogaville.ORG

www.swamisatchidananda.ORG

Dedication

This booklet is dedicated, with love and devotion, to our Beloved and Revered Sri Gurudev, His Holiness Sri Swami Satchidanandaji Maharaj, on the occasion of Guru Poornima 2004.

On this occasion we also celebrate the Silver Jubilee (25th Anniversary) of Satchidananda Ashram-Yogaville. It is through Sri Gurudev's Divine Grace and abundant Blessings that we are supremely fortunate to have the opportunity to be part of Satchidananda Ashram-Yogaville, his vision of heaven on earth.

May we all be blessed to live up to and fulfill that vision that Sri Gurudev has for each of us and for Yogaville. May the holy occasions of *Guru Poornima* and the Silver Jubilee of Yogaville inspire us to dedicate our hearts and lives more fully to the fulfillment of the dream.

Acknowledgments

To Sri Gurudev, with greatest respect and gratitude for his yogic example, for the teachings of Integral Yoga, and the cherished gift of the sanctified holy abode of Satchidananda Ashram-Yogaville.

We wish to thank Prakash Shakti Capen for her editing skills, Ananda Siva Hervé for designing the booklet, Sri Swami Yogananda for Sanskrit consultation, Abhaya Thiele for transcript research, Shakticom for recording Sri Gurudev's talks, Swami Muruganandaji for *Sastri* (the talk transcripts database), Karen Hogg for editiorial assistance, Terri Ward for transcript typing, Paraman and Lakshmi Barsel for editorial consulting, and Rev. Prem Anjali who served as production supervisor.

Special thanks to Amma Kidd (who served as a traveling secretary to Sri Gurudev soon after he arrived in the USA) for sharing her remembrances of the early years of Sri Gurudev's discussions about Yogaville.

We are extremely grateful for the generous gifts of these donors who made the publication of this booklet possible:

Mr. Vyra Karunananthan and family
Mr. and Mrs. Harry Wadhwani and family
The William and Margaret Feldman Foundation
Prajapati and Pushkari Swaine
Deepa and Param McNulty

Contents

Photographs of Yogaville

Preface
A Yogaville "Tour"

The Blue Ridge Mountains provide the perfect backdrop, and the rolling hills of rural Central Virginia offer the ideal setting for Satchidananda Ashram-Yogaville, Virginia. Sri Gurudev founded Yogaville as an optimal environment in which to study and live the principles of Integral Yoga. Now, 25 years later, that Yoga village continues to grow, still nurtured by his vibrant and enduring spirit.

Yogaville is a dynamic community where one finds people of varying ages and backgrounds enjoying all that the Ashram has to offer. In addition to the more than 2,000 guests and program participants who visit each year, 150 residents make this their home. There is a monastery for the swamis, as well as dormitories for guests and single residents, and many family homes nearby.

Visitors to Yogaville usually start at the Visitors' Center in Sivananda Hall. This is the place where everyone comes together for delicious vegetarian meals, community gatherings, and *satsangs*. Right across the lawn of the quadrangle are two dormitories, the warmly welcoming Guest Services department, and several classrooms. A wonderful, large, full-service library can be found in a building next to the dorms; Guru Bhavan, the peaceful meditation hall, stands on the opposite side.

Next to Guru Bhavan is the newest addition: The Integral Yoga Teaching Academy, which hosts more than 15 Teacher Training programs each year. In addition to Hatha Yoga and Meditation

Teacher Training programs, there is a wide variety of advanced and specialized certification courses such as: Cardiac Yoga,® Extra Gentle Yoga, Stress Management, Prenatal/Postnatal Yoga, Yoga for the Special Child,™ and Yoga for Cancer Patients.

Just a short walk away, the Lotus Guest Houses offer private rooms to guests. The little Lotus Tea House is a place to enjoy refreshments, good company, and internet access. There are plans to expand these facilities even further.

Back in Sivananda Hall are the offices of Shakticom, the full-service audio and video studio. The staff of Shakticom has recorded Sri Gurudev's programs for many years. They continue to produce tapes of these beautiful teachings and, also, tapes by disciples of Sri Gurudev. Shakticom, along with the Photo Department and the Archives, is actively involved in preserving the wealth of tapes and films collected from Sri Gurudev's service over many decades and in sharing these treasures with the public.

A left turn out of the Sivananda Hall parking area will take you to the nearby Office Building, which houses the Office of the President of the Integral Yoga organization, Swami Asokananda, and the administrative offices of Yogaville. The Office Building also contains the Ashram Reservation Center, the Yogaville Federal Credit Union, graphic design, and Integral Yoga Publications, among other indispensable departments.

It also includes the Programs Department, which plans more than 50 programs throughout the year. A sample of the week-long and weekend workshops include: seasonal Silent Retreats,

Meditation Retreats, Yoga and Psychotherapy, Self-Discovery through Hatha Yoga, Yoga Teachers' conferences, Interfaith programs, and Vegetarian Cooking courses. It is through these, and other programs, that guests have a chance to experience the "heaven on earth" that Sri Gurudev created in Yogaville. Many of the senior residents of Yogaville, in addition to enjoying the benefits of living in this wonderful spiritual community, enjoy sharing the teachings of Integral Yoga with others. The Yogaville *satsangs* and programs provide this opportunity.

The Office Building also houses the offices of the LYT (Living Yoga Training) program. The LYT program gives spiritual aspirants an opportunity to spend a month or more experiencing the unique environment of Yogaville, with the guidance and support of senior members and experienced teachers, and to participate in spiritual practices, activities, and Karma Yoga at the Ashram.

As longtime resident (and former Yogaville East president) Paraman Barsel shared, "One of the most beautiful things is how Sri Gurudev wanted everyone who came to Yogaville to feel welcome and that this was their spiritual home. Whether the person was here for a guest stay or for the Living Yoga Training, to take a retreat or a Teacher Training program, when it came time for them to leave, Sri Gurudev always said, 'Remember, you have a home here. You are always welcome here.' I believe that all those around the world who have been touched by Yogaville literally feel that this is their home and they can always come back home. And the reality is that when they do come, they are embraced by the people here."

Driving further down the main road, you come to Nectar Lane—the location of the only building that existed when Yogaville was initially established. This building is where Sri Gurudev first lived in Virginia, and was the home to the original residents. It was the site of the Ashram Temple and *satsang* hall, the dining hall, and offices. This building is now the Lotus Conference Center (LCC), which provides lodging, dining, and meeting room facilities for various programs including the Fine Arts Society (FAS).

The Fine Arts Society was first established in the 1950's in Sri Lanka by Sri Gurudev, assisted by Mrs. Rukmini (Amma) Rasiah. Sri Gurudev was dedicated to promoting the fine arts of music, dance, and drama in all their magnificent forms. In addition to its regular activities, the FAS also sponsors special summer *Bharata Natyam* dance camps and workshops for dance teachers. The Ananda Kala Mandir is located right next to the LCC; this is the main dance studio and performance hall for the FAS. Just behind the LCC is a panoramic overlook from which guests can view the Blue Ridge Mountains and the James River, as well as the Light Of Truth Universal Shrine (LOTUS).

Also on Nectar Lane is the office of Dr. Amrita Sandra McLanahan, our "Yoga M.D." For many years, Dr. McLanahan has been active in bridging the gap between conventional and alternative medicine.

Turning right out of the Sivananda Hall parking area, you find Sannyasi Nivas, the monastery where the swamis live. A little further is the Service Building, which contains the auto repair shop, maintenance workshop, and woodworking shop. It is also where the emergency vehicles for the Yogaville Fire Department and Rescue Squad are housed.

A little further down the road is Integral Yoga Distribution, a thriving business that distributes thousands of books, tapes, videos, and other Yoga and wellness-related items to nearly 10,000 bookstores, health food stores, Yoga centers, and individuals. Founded in 1986 in a small corner in the office building basement, Integral Yoga Distribution has grown into its own large building with a warehouse, a staff of 15, and bustling phone lines.

A few more feet down the main road is Karuna Road. In addition to the many private roads and subdivisions nearby where household residents have their own homes and some businesses, Karuna Road is the location of YOCOSO (the Yogaville Cooperative Society). This is land leased by the Ashram to householders where they have built homes.

At the end of Karuna Road, the visitor will find the Yogaville Vidyalayam to the left. From the earliest days, when Sri Gurudev began speaking about a Yoga village, there was a gleam in his eyes when he mentioned a school for children. Today, the Yogaville Vidyalayam (Temple of Learning) provides individual programs for children from ages 5 to 12. This private, nonprofit, parochial school is based on the precepts and teachings of Sri Gurudev, such as truth, nonviolence, dedication, universal brotherhood, interfaith understanding, and the multicultural approach. Sri Gurudev always said, "The purpose of the Vidyalayam is to turn out good people." We see again and again that our school is doing just that, as students go on to graduate from college with honors and follow their dreams into a variety of impressive professions.

The three shrines at Yogaville are the LOTUS, Kailash, and Chidambaram. Dedicated to the Light of all faiths and to world peace, the LOTUS is unique in the world. The LOTUS (pictured on the back cover) was conceived and designed by Sri Gurudev. The Shrine is built in the shape of a lotus flower, an ancient symbol for the spiritual unfoldment of the soul. Inside, each major world faith is represented by an altar. People of all paths are welcome to come and meditate or pray in silence. The Shrine is set amid the peace and calm of a 16-acre lake and is adorned with pools, waterfalls, and a grand cupola topped with a golden spire.

The highest point on the Yogaville property is the site known as Kailash, named after the holy abode of Lord Siva in the Himalayas. Siva Nataraja, the King of Cosmic Dance, dances within a flaming halo symbolizing the eternal Om. Through the generosity of Sri Dr. Karan Singh and his wife, Princess Yasho, a magnificent bronze statue of Lord Nataraja adorns the majestic hilltop overlooking the LOTUS.

During the mid-1980's, Sri Gurudev spoke more specifically about the time when he would leave the body. When his disciples asked how to best plan for this, he guided them in the construction of a building at Yogaville to house his body after his *Mahasamadhi* (a God-realized soul's conscious final exit from the body). This building was situated in perfect alignment between the LOTUS and Kailash according to Sri Gurudev's instructions. When asked what to call the building, he replied: "Chidambaram." In the heart of Tamil Nadu, there is an ancient Temple named Chidambaram. The deity worshipped in Chidambaram is the Lord Nataraja, Sri Gurudev's *Ishta Devata*.

Sri Gurudev took *Mahasamadhi* on August 19, 2002 in South India. Shortly before leaving the body, Sri Gurudev told many people: "I will always be with you in Spirit. Even if my body is not there, you will never be without me." That is the reason we do not refer to him as having died or passed away, but rather as having dropped or left the body. That is what our Yoga tradition teaches us about the ongoing relationship with one's Satguru.

Sri Gurudev's body was interred inside Chidambaram, Yogaville, according to elaborate Vedic rituals on August 22, 2002. Sri Gurudev spoke about the special blessings that would emanate from his *Mahasamadhi* Shrine. He told devotees, "When the day comes that I leave the body, you will be able to come here to receive the answers to your questions and the solution to your problems."

So beloved are these shrines, they are sometimes referred to as the heart of Yogaville. But, there is no one structure or department that can be given this title. The heart of Yogaville will always be the expansive teachings and living presence of Sri Gurudev.

For information on Yogaville® programs, the Integral Yoga® Teaching Academy, guest stays, and day visits, please phone: 1-800-858-YOGA or visit us online at www.yogaville.ORG.

YOGAVILLE

A Spiritual Community

A Model World of
Health and Harmony; Peace and Prosperity

"People are puzzled and worried about the future of the world. The future of the world shall be a heaven. And this is the beginning here." Swami Satchidananda

Foreword
A Vision Whose Time Had Come
By Amma Kidd

"Yes Amma, anything is possible. With faith everything is possible." I hurriedly jotted down Sri Gurudev's words, and I remember the scene as if it was yesterday. He was describing, in detail, some aspect of the yogic community he had envisioned for many years, a vision whose time had come and which the Invisible Hand had somehow destined to manifest and grace this American soil. Gurudev described it as a miniature model world, a model city, a model village, a "Yoga village," and, consequently, it was named "Yogaville."

This conversation took place in 1970 during our first Integral Yoga retreat held at Annhurst College. He continued: "Yogaville is to be a seed of heaven on earth to influence the earth to become a heaven. It can happen if we really want it! Once Yogaville is there, the conditions of life may not appear to be very different, but what will make it into a heaven is people coming together with the right understanding and the right attitude."

Over the next couple of years or so Sri Gurudev spoke almost continually and constantly about the vision of Yogaville. I say "the" vision and not "his" vision; because, before long, through the spiritual power imbuing his words, it had become our vision as well. It was as if he had thrown a magical crystal ball our way and we all—as one single body, one single being—had eagerly jumped to catch it!

Within the crystal ball, we could see Yogaville displayed in detail as Gurudev would describe it to us. He spoke of buildings: A building to house a school for children, a building for a common kitchen and a dining hall, a building for a hall for *satsangs* and other programs, a building for a guest house, a building for a cultural center run under yogic guidelines, a building for a bank, and so on. He talked about Yogaville having land for a vegetable garden, an orchard, and flower gardens.

He envisioned Yogaville as economically self-sustaining and spoke of cottage industries and a Yoga Academy. It is truly heart-warming to look around and see how much of this has already manifested right down to the opening of the new Integral Yoga Academy in 2004! And it is all happening in Sri Gurudev's typically unassuming, steady, natural way.

As the centerpiece of Yogaville and as a powerful statement of its meaning and purpose, he would describe the magnificent Light Of Truth Universal Shrine, or LOTUS. He explained the concept and had us each draw our ideas of the Shrine and present them to him. We all got fully engaged in this project. It was a most inspiring and beautiful vision within the crystal ball; after all, the ball was ours—he had gifted it to us!

As I did my little drawing, I remember feeling: "Wouldn't it be incredible if a small part of my drawing was incorporated into the LOTUS?" It was a thrilling thought! No doubt many others had similar feelings, but whether or not our concepts were incorporated was immaterial. In that bundle of papers containing our drawings, Gurudev was able to scoop up into his heart the love, enthusiasm and faith of our hearts; and that was the initial substance he was waiting for in order to start erecting the laudable monument to the Divine LIGHT: the LOTUS.

Following this pattern, when the time came to write a Charter for Yogaville, Sri Gurudev asked us to write down our concepts of what the document should say and present them to him. A Charter Committee was created and subdivided into small groups. My heart was not in it, and I wrote to Gurudev, saying: "I don't want to write anything for the Charter. I feel the Charter is something very sacred. We, who know much less than you, should not write the guiding principles—those should come from you."

I don't know if it was in answer to my heartfelt request, but the fact is that, soon afterward, he presented us with a handwritten final version of the Charter [see pages 48-49].

Yogaville is the result of Sri Gurudev's faith. It was created out of his faith, and he imparted that faith to us to the point that we thought, breathed, wrote, drew, talked, and lived Yogaville as an undisputed reality. In the early days, he had us organize into teams, and, on the weekends, we would go scouting various places around New York and other areas on the east coast, looking for land.

The fact that there was hardly any money in the bank account didn't faze us at all; we had no doubts. It was truly a manifestation of faith in action. Later, as the word spread, donations began to come in; and, in 1971, a beautiful property was found in Virginia, about 20 minutes from Charlottesville and about two hours from Washington, D. C.

Hari Zupan and I went with Gurudev to see the land. It was a beautiful farm with lots of buildings already on it. It seemed ideal. Gurudev got into a jeep and we drove all over the property. Gurudev loved it. We all met back in New York and sat together with Gurudev looking at slides of the property, and we decided to make an offer on the property.

For those who were new to the project, Hari Zupan gave an introduction: "The whole idea of Yogaville began when Sri Gurudev first came here, about five years ago. The need immediately became apparent for a place where spiritual aspirants, people who wanted to practice Yoga, could do so in a country setting, in a retreat setting. About four years ago, we looked in upstate New York for places that might suit this, a small piece of land for a country retreat.

Last year, shortly before Gurudev left for his recent tour around the world, he was talking about the idea of the ashram we have been seeking for so long, and he started saying, 'I don't just see a country ashram, now. I see a whole town, a Yoga town or a Yogaville.' So, from the point of view of an ashram—a place where people could go on weekends—the idea began to germinate for a year-round ashram, a place where people could live the whole week, the whole season, the whole year, and live a completely yogic life."

So, after many months of intense searching for the right property for Yogaville East, we all gave a joyous sigh of relief when the "perfect" land, with the "perfect" price, on the "perfect" location finally appeared. Groups followed groups to see the land, to feel it and to make plans. This was the realization of a dream of many years in the hearts of many—a dream very close to Sri Gurudev's heart. We were all full of expectancy as we neared the days on which the final papers were to be signed.

A very dear friend of mine came one day from New York to visit Gurudev. The three of us were sitting, having tea in the little lake house in Danbury, Connecticut that Gurudev occupied at the time. As we talked, a phone call came and Gurudev answered it, "Yes? Hmmm. Hm, hm. Wonderful. Aha...aha...Wonderful! I understand. That's fine. Yes. Wonderful! Thank you for calling. Om Shanthi, Shanthi."

The little tea party came to an end; and, after a pleasant afternoon, my friend departed. That evening, I was looking over some last minute business with Gurudev when he casually mentioned that we had lost the land. He said that something unexpected occurred, and the deal fell through.

"Oh my God, Swamiji, that's terrible. How could that happen? When did it happen? When did you hear about it?"

"This afternoon. It was that phone call that came while we were having tea, remember?"

"That phone call, Swamiji? But you sounded happy and I heard you say nothing but, 'Wonderful, wonderful!'"

He gave me a look between surprised and amused. Shrugging his shoulders, he merrily said, "Sure, Amma. When things come, good. When they go, wonderful!"

And that was that! At the last minute it was gone! In 1973, we purchased an estate in Pomfret, Connecticut. Finally, Yogaville was a palpable reality, a dream come true. Unbeknownst to us, Yogaville East was to be but the cradle for what was to unfold later.

While living there we transcended many challenges and hurdles in learning how to live together while applying the practical, spiritual principles of Yoga as taught by our Gurudev. He took part in every part of our lives, constantly coaxing, encouraging, guiding, and inspiring us. We followed as best as we could, aided by the fact that we were all on fire to become saints!

With overwhelming heating expenses due to harsh winters, and the rapid growth of the community with no room to expand in our present location, Gurudev again organized us into a land search. In 1979, destiny brought us back to Virginia, 45 miles south of Charlottesville. So, here we are 25 years later; and Sri Gurudev's vision is flourishing!

I vividly remember one day Sri Gurudev pulled up unexpectedly to Shanti Kutir and asked me to get into his car. He drove me all over Yogaville to places I knew well and others I didn't. All the while, I was wondering what it was all about. He drove all over, briefly stopping at each place. When the tour was over, he stopped the car before arriving at Shanti Kutir and said to me: "So now I have shown you everything. I am doing the best to leave everything, all the basic things, ready for them so that, when I leave this body, they won't have too much difficulty in developing it further. They can just continue. I am doing as much as I can. I am doing everything I can."

Often, while expounding some spiritual principles, Gurudev would say: "It is all up to you." Sri Gurudev has given us everything. It is up to us to cherish his invaluable legacy, knowing that—as long as we depend on his Grace—he will be able to use us as instruments to expand his vision in order to bless this world. We are indeed supremely blessed!

Sri Gurudev's Vision of Yogaville

YOGAVILLE: a community of people rising, as individuals and as a group, above man-made differences in order to experience the joy and peace of genuine living.

YOGAVILLE: a haven for all religions. A place to stay, meditate and pray. Everyone welcome. All religions, all differences accepted.

YOGAVILLE: a dedication to God.

YOGAVILLE: a place to realize the True Self through the acts of everyday life.

YOGAVILLE: an embrace to all nations, cultures and creeds.

YOGAVILLE: an opportunity to improve the overall quality of life, in unity, peace and prosperity.

YOGAVILLE: an awakening!

YOGAVILLE: the Light of the future shining in the present.

(Comments made over several years, recorded by Amma Kidd)

Introduction

The goal of Yoga is to live a healthy, easeful, peaceful life, and a useful life. The aim is to help you to be always serene, peaceful, happy and, then, to be useful to others. The real spiritual experience is living together happily as one beautiful family with love. Yogaville is this one little miniature world where we are trying to prove that people from various places can come and live together harmoniously as one family.

Some people ask me, "I haven't realized God, I haven't had any experience. What is it that I have been practicing all these years?" I don't know what experience they want. Is it that they haven't lifted up from the ground or had some hallucination? That is not the spiritual experience I want. You may have some good visions, you may see some lights, hear some sounds, all right. What is the benefit to others? The real experience is to move around with smiling faces, loving faces. That is spiritual—see the spirit in others, love everybody, rise above the lower nature that's based on egoism. That is the real spiritual experience.

You may be regular in your practice. Every morning you come for one whole hour, you sit still, without any movement in meditation. But, if the minute you go out you express all your negative feelings to others, what is the use then? That is not spiritual practice. Be aware of any animosity, back-biting, dislikes, hatred. Imagine how happy you would be if you think, "Everybody loves me." That is what Yoga is in practical life—the application of your religious thoughts. The purpose of Yogaville is for that.

We are striving to live as a good community of Yogis according to the yogic principles. Our goal is to make a beautiful Yogaville community and to prove to the world that, as Yogis, we can live healthily, happily. If we can't make this little world a happy place to live, a harmonious place to live, there is no point in talking about global harmony or global peace. Please remember that. All of us should never forget: "My purpose in coming here is to make Yogaville a heaven, nothing less than that."

A heaven on earth means that your thoughts, feelings, speech, and actions are all yogic. Everything should be heavenly, heavenly, heavenly. Every individual has an important part to fulfill toward this goal. So, please remember it and work hard. Where there is a will there is a way. If we want, we can always make it; and God is there to help us. He is very kind, very generous in helping us this far; and I am sure He will continue to help. If we take one step toward that goal, He will come ten steps toward us. Let's do it.

Make sure that your life is a great contribution toward that. You should feel that, "I am part of this. I have a duty. I have a commitment to make this a heaven. I will do everything possible. If I really cannot do it, I won't mar it. I will simply say, 'Sorry, I am not yet ready for it. When I am ready, I will come back.'" Living here and being unhappy and miserable, is against our principles.

It is not just for me you are doing this. And I am not doing it for you. We are all together. We just want to prove something to the world—we are as one family. We came from various places, we have various tastes, temperaments, beliefs, but we are living here as one family. When I go out, around the globe, I say, "If you want to see a heaven, come to Yogaville."

Chapter 1–My Vision of Yogaville

My vision of Yogaville is a little heaven on the earth. It is a village filled with people who follow the yogic principles. Everything conducive to Yoga will be seen there. Our goal is to make a beautiful Yoga community. If we can't make this little world of ours a happy and harmonious place to live, there is no point in talking about global harmony or global peace.

Heaven is a place where love—and nothing but love—flows. There, we see real cosmic, universal love. Everybody is tied to that cosmic love. People love each other as they would love themselves. People love the animals, the plants, and all the things around them. People love even their trash cans. That's heaven. And they all live as one big family. There is no "mine and yours." There is only "ours." It's God's home, and all feel that they are just children in that home.

It's a collective life. Like parts of the same body, cells of the same body. Even if one part gets hurt all other parts will look into it. If your toe gets hurt, your eyes will immediately look into that. Your hands will go there to clean the wound. Every part takes care of that. Like that, even if one individual is unhappy, everybody will take care of that person and see that he or she becomes happy again. That is what you call a heaven. Our properties are common; our money is common; our kitchen is common; our school is common. In a way, everything belongs to everybody. That's how people live in heaven. If we can live that way, certainly we will make a heaven here.

That is exactly what the yogic life means—living a collective life, rising above the little, self-centered life. We share the joy of everybody; we share the pain of everybody. If even one is hurt, everybody should feel the hurt.

Our humble ambition in Yogaville is this: Let us make a better world in our miniature world here. Let us give up selfishness. Let us learn to live clean, healthy, happy lives. Let's not allow anything that could disturb our physical health or mental peace. We believe in doing things that will bring us health and happiness. By keeping ourselves healthy and happy, we are preparing ourselves to offer our service to the larger community around us.

Living an ashram life doesn't mean that you separate yourself from the world, go into seclusion and ignore the world. Not at all. In fact, an ashram is a ground to prepare yourself for it. In an ashram, you become fit to serve the world. We want a better world, but it's impossible to transform the whole world overnight. We have to start somewhere.

Where should your world begin? Right around you. Yoga begins at home. The Yogaville land, by itself, is always heavenly. Wherever you go, God has created only heavenly places. But, to see the heavenly abode, we need that kind of eye, that kind of mind. Hell and heaven are in your own mind. You can make it into a heaven.

If you are not peaceful, you cannot bring peace to others. If you are not a Yogi, you cannot spread Yoga. It's not only charity that begins at home; even divinity begins at home. Everything begins at home. If you become a better person, that part of the world becomes better.

Of course, that doesn't mean that you should not do anything for other parts of the world. Do it. But, at the same time, do something right in and around you. That is the most important part. If you want to help others, you have to equip yourself first.

In our own humble way, Yogaville is a small starting point for a better world. Yogaville is a place to learn to embrace the entire universe with the idea that God has a purpose for everybody. Nobody is superior; nobody is inferior. We are all doing God's work. We are all working together for a goal. We are learning to share and care, love and give.

Building up a whole village is not that easy. Certainly, as a single individual, I cannot do anything. I look forward to all of your support, energy, goodwill. Maybe, one day, you will come to be citizens of Yogaville. If everything goes according to our present plan, we will have a township of our own with a yogic mayor with a Yoga police, Yoga fire service, more Yoga doctors. Yes, everything Yoga. God is giving us all that.

Remember that it is not built for one or two individuals. It is built for everybody. So, all of you should take as much interest as possible. Don't just come for the Saturday *satsang*, sit, listen, and go. Everybody should think of Yogaville and do whatever you can in whatever way. It is a big project. Our aim is that we want this as a sort of exemplary world which we are all looking for.

It is easy to say that we want a peaceful world. Mahatma Gandhi called it *Rama Rajayam*. That means, The Kingdom of Rama. In the Kingdom of Rama, there is no fighting; there is no theft; there is no crime. Everything is beautiful. No animosity. Even the animals that would normally fight play together. A beautiful world, a heaven.

How would that heaven be? Everybody will be loving and happy together. We can make a heaven like that. If we can't make a heaven in this little place, then, what is the point of talking about a peaceful, heavenly world everywhere?

That is what our Father in the heaven looks for from all of us. Let us make the Father proud. Let us make His creation a better place to live and enjoy. Every one of us should put forward our best effort to make this little world a happy place. Mere talking will not take us anywhere. Let us act and set examples. Let people learn from your example.

We can make Yogaville a better place, a heavenly place so that people can feel that great vibration, that great energy. When they go home, let them take some of that energy with them. People who come here will feel the health and peace. The place will be filled with healthy vibrations, with nothing to pollute those vibrations. If you like, you can let the seeds that grow there spread out, so that one day you will see the whole world as a big Yogaville. May such a thing happen soon. May more people learn to be Yogis. That is my sincere wish and prayer. So let us do it. Let us change ourselves, and then change the whole world into a beautiful heaven.

Chapter 2–The Light at the Center

Every village should have a temple. First, you build the temple and then live around the temple. This was the teaching of the great old saintly lady, Avvaiyar. She said, "Never live in a village where there is no temple." That was her commandment. That means God is the Lord of the village. We are all God's subjects. So, the Light Of Truth Universal Shrine will be the palace for that king, for God. That is the dream that seems to be haunting me.

The main reason for all the unrest in the world, I feel, is the lack of proper understanding of the spiritual side of the people. I'm trying to bring an awareness that, only through faith, can we help people to realize their spiritual oneness. The moment people understand their spiritual oneness, there is peace. The scriptures say that peace is really in realizing the oneness.

Before I even started building the LOTUS, I did some serious thinking, "Is it necessary? Should we spend money for that? Why can't we spend that money for the more needy people who need something immediately?" And people sometimes ask me these questions. My answer is that I don't deny the importance of immediate service to those who are needy, poor, sick and hungry. But why are people poor? Why are they sick? Why are they hungry? Treating a disease is good, but treating the cause is more important.

The world is destroying itself in the name of religion: "Mine is the best, yours is the worst." The Hindus and Muslims. The Sikhs and the Hindus. The Jews and the Christians. Fighting, fighting. Is that what the religion is? Do you think God will be happy? No. God wants all His children loving each other, playing with each other, even when they follow different paths. That is why I wanted to build the LOTUS.

The LOTUS will draw many people because it is something unique in the whole world. LOTUS is one of a kind. There is no other shrine like this, accommodating all the various chapels under one roof.

The other day, someone sent me a small clipping about a church in California where there is a Catholic and a Protestant chapel under one roof. Here, we are putting all the world religions under one roof. In that respect, it is unique. It should be the pride of Yogaville.

All the religions coming together, respecting each other is Yoga in religion. To bring the religions together is LOTUS. To bring the people together is Yogaville. That is why LOTUS is a part of Yogaville. We are trying our best to reach the people and to tell them that peace is the most important thing. Without peace, even if you have gained the whole world, it is of no use.

Our religion in Yogaville could be called, "Undoism." Enough damage has been done to nature and humanity in the name of religion and God. It is time to undo that. Look at history: More people were killed in the name of God and religion. Even wars and other calamities didn't kill so many people.

That's why, you may call it any way—Hindu or Undo or Christian or Buddhist or Jewish or no religion. Our religion is the basic foundation of all the religions, all the faiths. What we practice is found in every faith, every religion.

That means we want to be good and do good. We are be-gooders and do-gooders. We want our lives to be easeful and peaceful so that we can be useful. That is our religion.

We don't say people should give up their chosen religion. No. Never, never, never. We don't believe in that kind of conversion. Just because I love my mother, should I ask you to renounce your mother and love my mother? I should know that as I love my mother, you also love your mother. So we say, "Let us each love our mothers." There is no need to give up your own. In fact, you should not. Be loyal to your parents, your religion, your country; but, at the same time, love the other fellow's also.

You don't have to renounce this to love somebody. That's why it is a universal approach. It is not uniformity, but universality—unity in diversity. We are not trying to put everything into one religion.

The world is really beginning to understand this now. There are many, many global interfaith conferences. The time has come; the world has shrunk. We cannot separate ourselves and deny each other. It's time to know, respect, love one another and to live as one global family. Our humble aim in building the LOTUS is to spread that message.

Chapter 3–Yogaville: Its Real Purpose

I ask you to build yourselves as good Yogis. That is the purpose for which you are here. You are here to attain the highest knowledge—the knowledge of God, of your own true nature, the true Self within. Your purpose is to know your Self. But, you won't know your Self unless you see your Self; because seeing is believing. If you want to see your true Self you should have a clean mirror, which is the mind.

When you go in front of a mirror what do you do? You put on some makeup. You want to make your face beautiful. Do you apply all the powders to the mirror? No. You stand in front of it so you can see your face. But, you don't change the mirror. You look in the mirror to see where to apply the makeup, to see what is to be corrected.

Yogaville is a mirror, a big mirror. There, you see your image. It reflects your own impurities. If you don't like something, that means you are not liking yourself. If you get upset with something, you are upset with yourself. Nobody in this world, nothing in this world, can make you happy or unhappy. If we don't learn how to do that on our own, the world is going to teach us—in a hard way. God has placed a mirror right in front of you, the mirror of your mind. You came to enjoy life—the joy of living a dedicated life. Nothing, nothing, nothing can bring that joy to you other than total dedication.

So, either be intelligent and learn it yourself or learn by your own troubles and difficulties in the world. Either way, we are learning, no doubt. But the sooner we learn, the better will be our lives. And the world will be better too.

The purpose of Yoga and of living in an ashram is to help you know your own true nature, true Self within. You are the Knower. You are the Self, but you have forgotten who you are. You identify with the "doer." You may question, "Then, why do you ask me to go and dig the ground? I want to experience God."

To prepare yourself to experience God you have to clean out all the impediments that are in the way. So, while you pull the weeds outside, you are pulling the weeds in the mind. When you remove the rock, you are taking out the rocks inside. That is the meaning, the purpose of Karma Yoga.

Doing your practices (asana, *pranayama*, meditation) alone is not enough. Keep watching your mind. See whether it is balanced, whether it is free from selfishness. In that way, you are always happy, healthy, peaceful, joyful. That is why we have all these various activities in Yogaville.

Behind all these activities there is a purpose. You should feel, "They are giving me an opportunity to clean myself up. They are all helping me to grow. Let them do whatever they want and help me grow." If you have that attitude, then it becomes a heaven to you. If you can't find a heaven here, you are not going to find a heaven wherever you go.

All these activities are to give you an opportunity to get rubbed and scrubbed. They are all a part of Karma Yoga. Remember, if you want to call yourself a Yogi and a Karma Yogi, anything and everything that you do should be a joy to you. If you make faces and do it, you are poisoning that activity. Nobody forces you to do that. You should enjoy what you do. You should know you are doing it for your benefit. Then you are a Yogi.

All our activities here are not even to establish anything outside. That is an excuse. Building Yogaville, building LOTUS, building Sivananda Hall, paving the road. All kinds of activities. I think the world can live without any of these things. Our first and foremost duty is to build ourselves. And how would you build yourself? When you clean up your room, you are cleaning up your heart. When you remove the mess on the table, you are clearing the mess within you. Every outside action should be transformed into personal, inside action. Take it as yours, do it for your sake.

Don't run away because there is a little friction. Don't jump out. Stay put. Be strong. However rough it is. Don't think that the minute someone walks in they are changed overnight. No. We all come with our own situations, difficulties, problems. We are not enforcing any label—like you have to be a Catholic, a Protestant, a Buddhist, a Hindu, or anything else. You don't have to be anybody with a label. But you have to be a part of Yogaville.

So, please remember this always. Everybody should have a tape of this. Listen, listen, listen constantly. Because I am watching. I am not always happy about the attitudes I see. Some do not want to get cleaned out; they want to jump out of the wok before they get fried. It will be your loss if you jump out.

It's also easy to throw somebody out, but we are here not for that. Whoever wants to come, at least that person has the feeling of coming in and living here. With all the defects, it doesn't matter. We are all here to help each other. Keep that one, big aim in mind always. It's easy to theorize. We can talk for hours and hours, months and months, years and years. That won't help us. We have to apply it in practice.

The process of cleaning up the mind is almost like the relationship between an owner and their pet. The "doer" is your pet, a nice little puppy. Now, you try to train the puppy. It jumps at you, licks at your face; and it doesn't listen to you. What would you do? How would you train it? You would send it to a bad dog school. As simple as that. So, if the knower cannot control the doer, send it to the bad dog school. Satchidananda Ashram-Yogaville, Virginia is such a school.

Of course, in this case it's not that somebody else takes care of it. Somebody will help you to make yourself strong; and, then, he'll teach you how to take care of your own puppy. You can learn the art of training your puppy. Yogaville is also like a big laundromat. Bring all your dirty linen here. It will all get washed out. There will be a lot of rubbing and scrubbing.

It may be painful to the linen. But, if you know the purpose—that you are cleaning up your ego—then it will not be as painful. You will welcome the process because you know the purpose and you want the benefit.

If you like to get it corrected, get it corrected. It is for your benefit. It is not for the sake of anyone else. Sometimes we come across people who come and live here thinking that, "Oh, I am doing it for somebody's sake." No. You don't have to do for others' sake. If you think that you are doing it for others' sake, you don't have to, you can go. You are not a hired employee here, or a servant, or a paid laborer.

We come here not to do things for others. Sometimes I see people with the attitude that they are doing it for me, for my sake. I don't like that idea. I can just be a symbol here, that is all; but don't do it for my sake. If you are going to do it for my sake, you won't be doing it for long.

Do it for your sake. Sometimes people even said to me, "If you like, I'll do it." Why should you do it if I like? If I like, I will do it; I won't wait for you. You may never do it to my liking. If I really like to do something I will do it myself. For whose sake are you doing? For your sake.

Did we invite you? You wanted to come. We have given you an opportunity to come, so that you can do things to clean up yourself. That is why we are here. That is the purpose of Yogaville.

Our main challenge is when our personal interests come to distract us. Our past *samskaras* pop in. Very soon, we forget why we came here. If you could just have written down why you came here first of all, what brought you here, you would even be ashamed of yourself now. "See, I came for that purpose. What am I doing now? I've totally forgotten my original purpose. All I am thinking about is a little comfortable room, a little tasty food, a little less work, and more money." Very soon we forget. That is the big obstacle.

No one brought you here by force. No. You came yourself, voluntarily. Maybe you didn't realize how hard it is to clean up. You might even think, "Hmmm. If I had known this before…" But, unfortunately, you are already in the hot pot, you cannot jump out. That's what. Remember the goal. Always keep the goal in mind.

That is ashram life. To polish a stone, you rub it against another stone. And, while this stone gets polished, the other one also gets polished. That is what is happening here. We all come here as rough stones, and we rub against each other, make too much noise; but, in the process, all of us get softened. It is a complete healing process. If we remember this, there is a beautiful harmony.

Harmony doesn't mean that everything always goes smoothly. In the midst of turmoil there should be harmony. In the midst of a lot of rubbing there should be harmony. In the midst of the operation—chopping and cutting and stitching—there should be harmony.

And that's possible only when you always remember this: "I have an ultimate aim behind this." The minute we forget, we are against each other. "Who are you to tell me anything? It's none of your business!" If you don't want to get rubbed and polished, then probably you are not ready for this kind of life. You are not interested in bringing a heaven on earth.

Day and night think of it, dream of it, and never forget it. Without that, we cannot really build a Yogaville. I'm counting on every one of you. It doesn't matter whether you are a swami or a householder or little child or a big one. The purpose should not be forgotten. Our one and only purpose here is to get rubbed against each other, get smoothed out so that there will be complete harmony.

I would ask all the people who live here to remember this. That's why we are here. We are here to rub against each other and get polished. That is the purpose of an ashram. If we can't accomplish this here, the entire purpose will be lost. It's not for business and buildings and preaching we are here. We don't have to preach.

When people walk in they should see something special. They should see that all of you have been smoothed out. We have come here to build a heaven on earth—nothing less than that. Don't give up. Rome was not built in a day. It doesn't matter whether we achieve it tomorrow, the day after, or next year, or ten years after. Everyone should remember that goal.

You may not become a saint overnight. Even though, within yourself, you may have a little friction—some problems here and there—at least for the others, strive to be more saintly. If you have any negative feeling about anybody, think of it now. By this evening that should be out of your heart.

We sometimes have to act as saints at first, even though we are not really feeling that way. If we imitate to be great Yogis and saints and sages, we'll become that. There is a story of a thief who was sitting under the king's bedroom. He heard the king telling his ministers that his daughter was going to marry a saintly man. The king listed all the qualities of this saintly man. The thief listened so intently and became an imitator. Eventually, he became a real saint. As you think, so you become. So, imitate at least. Keep imitating.

Daily you have to question, "Who brought me here? Nobody. I came myself. What for? Am I keeping that goal in front of me? Am I marching toward that?" I know that if any one of you were out in the world you could be probably be making millions of dollars now.

So, if you don't have that yogic goal in mind, why are you wasting your time here? Why did you leave all that and come here? What for? You have to question. If you make a fuss when you are not given the exact food that you expected, who stops you? Go ahead, go out there to all the nice restaurants. Eat whatever you want.

See, the problem is the mind has that tendency. It makes you easily forget your goals. Constantly keep the mind focused on that. That is the purpose of Yogaville. Always remind yourself, "I have come here for my benefit. Anything I do benefits me. I am not here to do anything for others."

It takes work for a boxer to be a big boxing champion. What does he do? He goes and hits something, a pillow-like thing. Why is he hitting the pillow? Is he interested in making the pillow stronger? By hitting the pillow his muscles get strengthened. Likewise, you are hitting challenges here to make yourself strong, physically, mentally, and spiritually.

How can you make yourself stronger? Your diet may be a pure, yogic diet. Your practices may be very regular—you may meditate for an hour, three times a day. You do all the asanas, all the *pranayama*. But, what good of that if you cannot keep the mind calm and serene and loving and compassionate? That's what.

A mind should be free from all this nonsense—the junk, the dirty laundry. That saps a lot of our immunity. That is a wastage of *prana*. The biggest drain is our negative thinking.

A body and mind should have a good defensive force, a good immune system. That is the proof of Yoga. Not that I say outside influence, polluted air or polluted water or whatever it is would not affect you. Your body and mind are part of nature; they will get affected. But, immediately, there should be a healthy response from within. If not, that means there is something wrong with the defense system. You have to do everything to build it up.

And the worst drainage of your immune system is not just by your lack of exercise or diet, though they are all important. The most important drainage is what Gurudev Sivananda used to call "the rat holes." When a cultivator irrigates the land, if there are too many rat holes, all the water will go through the holes; and the crops will not get even a drop of water.

What is the rat hole that drains our life completely? The disturbing thoughts. Constantly thinking disturbing thoughts. Either about somebody or about yourself. The mind is the worst thing if it allows itself to be disturbed.

I want Yogaville to be totally immune to all these bugs that disturb the body and mind. No bugs should get into this territory. Yes, as it passes the junction of Route 604 the mental bugs should know, "Oh boy, there is something strong here. I can't get in." That's what. Not only you can make your body and mind immune and perfectly healthy, you can make the whole

Yogaville healthy. Yogaville is a bigger body, and you are all cells of that body. So, don't sell your cells by allowing dirty laundry to come in.

Remember we are all cells of the same body that we call Yogaville. Even if one cell gets contaminated, it will ruin the entire body. So, make your thoughts beautiful; be a fitting cell, a part of this body. That is why we are here—not just to come together and have a little fun and go away. You want to make it a permanent abode of peace and joy. Nothing less than that. And, of course, it's not possible without the help of each one of you.

Even one rotten apple, they say, will ruin the whole basket. But I don't always agree with that proverb. If all other apples are good, why can't they convert the rotten apple into a good apple? In the midst of all the beautiful people, even a thief, even a *rogi* (a diseased person) should become a Yogi.

Health, health, health, health. Don't worry about the world. You don't have to go and save the world right away. Save yourself first. Let's cooperate; the strategy of cooperation should begin right here. Yogaville is our moon, our Mars, our Neptune. Everything is here. At least one area can be absolutely free from all these unhealthy things.

It's not that we are building Yogaville for somebody else somewhere. No. You don't have to show to the world that, "Here, we have built a Yogaville." It is for our own sake. We are simply keeping a special place where we can grow—a fertile soil and a protected environment until we grow.

We are like tender plants. When you plant a new one, a young plant, you immediately have to put a fence around. Otherwise, even the charming, nice, good-looking deer will come and eat away. You like deer; at the same time you don't like them coming and eating the plants. So, you can't kill them. You want to have the deer and the plant. What would you do? You put a high fence around the tender plant so that the deer won't come and bite it.

Yogaville is like that. We are trying to keep it as protected as possible for us to grow. Once you grow, you don't even need the protection. Probably, you will become the mender of the fence then, so other young plants can grow.

We all should have that in mind: "I am proud to be in Yogaville, and I'll make Yogaville proud by my being here." We talk about "heaven on earth," "heaven on earth." Good heaven! Keep up that spirit. Think of it everyday, at least a little. "What am I doing to make this a better place?" Before you go to sleep, think of it. "Did I make this place a little better today?" Nothing is impossible. Where there is will there is way. But it needs a lot of effort, diligent actions. Easy to break. Hard to build up. Let us build it up.

If we always remember this truth, we will enjoy every minute of our presence here. That is the purpose of Yogaville. That way, Yogaville will bestow everything to you—everything that you need to make your life healthy, happy, and holy. We are not looking for a big quantity, thousands of members. We are not in a hurry to say, "Oh, Yogaville has thousands of Yogis here." If we have even ten good Yogis, that's more than enough, we have accomplished something. I wish you all the strength. God bless you.

Chapter 4–Let Us Walk Together

The purpose of Yogaville is to live together to help ourselves and each other find the peace and ease. As individuals, we may find it hard to achieve that end; so, collectively, we are helping each other. That is the goal.

Like-minded people living together, helping each other. When one slips, there should be ten others to pull the person up. That is the great benefit of *satsang*, the good company—you are placing yourself in a proper atmosphere. And, that is the very reason why we wanted Yogaville.

If you want to be a *Jivanmukta*, where do you begin? Change your company. Get to *satsang*. If you have good company, you are not in the bad company; that is the immediate benefit. Then, because you are not in the bad company, your mind is more calm. Because your mind is more calm, you experience your own inner Self. It is as simple as that.

The good company paves the way step by step, until at last you realize your own Self. You learn to be a *Jivanmukta*. Acharya Shankara beautifully presents this fact: "*Satsangatve nissangatvam, nissangatve nirmohatvam, nirmohatve nischalitatvam, nischalitatve jivanmuktih*. If you want to have the attainment of a *Jivanmukta*, if you want to get liberated from the clutches of ego, start with *satsang*."

Not everyone can do the right things all by themselves. On their own, there is nobody to encourage them toward the right. On the other hand there are so many people to pull you into the old life. Smoking, drinking, drugs, non-vegetarian diet, illicit sex. If you say, "I don't drink anymore" or "I don't take drugs anymore," your old friends will wonder what kind of abnormality you have developed!

Suppose you are a smoker, and you want to stop smoking. What would you do? Will you have friends who smoke a lot? Even though you want to do good things you might not be able to if you are in the wrong company.

If you have friends who smoke a lot, they will tempt you. They will wait for a weak moment to convince you to do that. So, shun that company and join the good company, the non-smokers. That is what is called *satsang*, the good company.

Join the good company; get on board of the ship. Then, even though, sometimes, your past experience will want you to put your hand in the pocket and take up a cigarette, fortunately you are in the good company. You feel ashamed to do that. So, you are separating yourself from all those things.

Good company will naturally, even without your effort, take you toward your goal. You are made by the company you keep. That is one of the main reasons why an ashram life, a protected and clean environment, is necessary.

An ashram is a sort of shallow-water swimming. It is a protected environment. Others are there not to drown you but to help you. If you go out into the regular life, you are getting into deep water; nobody will even bother to help you.

On the other hand, they may even push you down a little more. Here, it is shallow water. If, even in the shallow water, you are about to drown, there are hundreds of people to pull you out. The very purpose of community life is this.

Those who find it difficult to follow any spiritual practices don't have to do anything; just get onto the bandwagon. Change the environment; find the good company. That is the purpose of Yogaville. The moment you come and live here, many of the vices just drop away. Because there's no similar vibrations here, you won't even think of it. There are people to help you. That is one of the reasons we are developing Yogaville.

Many of our children are being born in Yogaville. Certainly, they must have been good Yogis before; they didn't finish their practices then, and they were looking for a Yoga home to continue. In a way, that is what we are trying to create here—a good Yoga home, a Yoga village—so that we can attract all those little, little Yogis who didn't finish their job. They can come over here and be born here in Yogaville.

The Vidyalayam is not just another school. It is the ancient *gurukulam* style. Living with the gurus. To see our little toddlers all grown up is wonderful. It's really a great task to be able to swim against the current. Often, I thought, "Will we survive?" but the children have proved it. Yes, with proper support and cooperation, we can achieve what we want. And we see the fruit of it today. My heart is filled with emotions when I think of these children, these young people.

Our main purpose here in Yogaville is to learn to live a clean life, a healthy life, a peaceful life. Anything that would adversely affect our physical health and mental peace should not be allowed to come in. In this age, it's very hard to build good character after the children grow up.

Discipline, good manners, good character, proper lifestyle—all this can be built only now, when they are young. That is why I have given lifestyle guidelines for the children and also for the adults. Follow these guidelines; they are for your benefit. You know what disturbs your mental or physical health. So, see the guidelines and then you decide yourself.

There are some very good programs on television. There is nothing wrong in watching TV. But what to watch? There are some wonderful books; but there are also books that are not fit for reading. Should we say nobody should read books? Study what is to be studied, or read what is to be read. Not everything is readable. The same way, not everything is seeable. The same way not everything is enjoyable. You know what is good and what is not good.

This is nothing new. Maybe for this age it is new. Thousands of years before, they knew about the effect of sound vibration on the body and the mind. All the chants and mantras have a positive effect. That is why you have nice, beautiful soft music like Gregorian chants and other things when you go to the church.

In general, we say that anything that's not violent, anything that's soft and serene is recommended. That is why I used one term "*sattwic*." Food must be *sattwic*, music must be *sattwic*. We just keep that as a guideline; and, then, you decide which TV show, what movies, and what music is good for you. It is not only for the children; these recommendations are for the grownups as well. If the grownups don't follow the guidelines, you can't blame the children.

So, if you are interested in the welfare of the children, the grownups also should follow it. If you can't, then you are not even following Yogaville principles. This is not the place for you then. In fact, when it comes to the level of affecting the children, I am going to be very strict about that.

Even the grownups should not play any agitating music or watch any TV that is not conducive for the children. Soft, gentle, nice parties are okay. Keep this as the guideline: "Anything that would adversely affect my body and mind is to be avoided." That's all. Have fun in the best way, the healthy way.

It is our duty to make Yogaville a Yogaville, not a "rogaville," please. Dating, yes, I have no objection to that. What is the meaning of dating? And at what stage? Strictly speaking, for the young people, until you finish your studies, there should be no dating. Your dating is with your books; because you are a student.

When you are ready to become a householder, sure, you can select a partner, get to know the partner. That getting to know the partner is what you call dating, and that happens only when you finish your school. Remember, studying means you are single, you are a student, no dating. Student life is student life.

For the adults, we are not asking that the single people should always remain single. If you want to find a partner, that is all right. Where else can you find a better boy or a better girl than in Yogaville? All who come here have one thing in mind: Yoga. We are not saying that you should not look for a partner and get married. But the guideline here is: Stick to one person.

We don't deny couples; but you should not be dating, dating, endlessly dating. There are some people who may feel, "Well, this is America. I might want to live with this girl for a week; then, if I don't like her, I'll go with somebody else, and then somebody else." No, that is almost like being at the grocery store and picking up this fruit and then that fruit while taking small bites. Get to know each other. Nothing wrong with that. But, within a limit. It's better to get into the married life if you don't want to be single.

Who says that married life is no good for spiritual practice? In fact, in married life you can easily become spiritual fast. There is a lot of rubbing and scrubbing in marriage. Instead of cleaning yourself, you have somebody to clean you up.

Marriage is a school. *Grihasta darshana* (householder path) is an important part. *Brahmachari*, *Grihasta*, *Vanaprasta*, *Sannyasi*. One has to go through the stages of life, step by step. So, go ahead, but do it within the guidelines.

If you don't want to get married right away, okay then you can have the Vow of Intent. You will be living like husband and wife. You make a commitment to each other; and, maybe after a year or two, you get married. But, there's one condition: In the process of living together, if the woman gets pregnant, as soon as you know it, you should get married.

Because we are not just having a sort of wild community here. No. I have faith in some principles, and I want to live up to that. I want all those people who have faith in those principles and want to live up to them.

If you have any doubt in my principles, question me. If I am wrong, I am ready to change. Until then, yes, my principles should be followed here.

If you don't want to follow the Ashram guidelines, do your own thing. Did we say to you, "Please come to Yogaville" No. You came yourself. What for? To get some benefit by being here. To refine your life. To clean up the mess. So, as long as you are here, follow the guidelines.

Otherwise, go out, get burned, and you'll drop all the bad habits by yourself. We're not objecting to that, but not here. In the old days, when you went on a plane, they asked you, "Do you want a smoking seat or a non-smoking seat?" If you are a non-smoker, sit in the non-smoking section. If you want to smoke, go to the smoking section.

So, this is non-smoking. If you know that people are not happy with your mentality or habits, change them. You didn't come to ruin the harmony here. If you can't follow the guidelines, you are free to go. Do it somewhere else. As long as you are here, follow the guidelines.

I'm not forcing you. When you know something is not right, drop it immediately. You can do it. But, if you don't want to do that, you can live in another place and come visit us now and then as a guest.

If you are calling yourself Yogaville community members, *sangha*, I insist that you should follow the guidelines. I am not going to give even a little room for that. Either we keep it clean and yogic or we close it. I'm very positive about that, and you should all understand the benefit. Don't ever do anything just because I say so. You should feel convinced yourself.

Yogaville is for those who want to experience an easeful, peaceful, and useful life. If I want to be peaceful, how can I be negative? How can I disturb somebody's peace? The cause of disturbed peace is a selfish attitude. The "I, me, mine." That is why we say in Yogaville there is no "I, me, mine." It is ours. We are all in a boat together. Either we float across or we sink together. There is a responsibility for everybody on the boat, to make the ship sail safely.

Chapter 5–Dedicate Your Life

Building Yogaville needs the beautiful cooperation of every individual. There needs to be a lot of loving and giving. It needs plenty of understanding, cooperation, coordination to live together as good Yogis.

Let us all learn to live a life of selflessness. Every one of you should feel that you are part of this family, the Yogaville family: "I'm living for the sake of this family. I'm living to make this Yogaville family a successful one. That is my goal." Think that way.

When you go sit, meditate, do your practices, even that should not be just for yourself but for the sake of the entire Yogaville. Anything and everything that could make Yogaville a success should be done by you. So, brush aside all your petty little demands and commands and egos. Know that you are here living for Yogaville. That is my request to make Yogaville a success. Think that way. Giving yourself completely to that.

I know it is very difficult. Even in one single family, where there may be five or six members born of the same womb, they don't always get along well. Here, we have plucked people from various trees, from various walks of life. To put them together and make them one family is difficult. But that is worth doing. We have to give up many of our individual idiosyncrasies.

Always think in terms of the whole: "How can we make this a beautiful place?" We may have to sacrifice many of our own personal ideas, but it's worth it. Sacrifice means to chop off our ego. For the benefit of everybody, you have to sacrifice something of your own.

We do have our independence and our individuality, but our individuality should not interfere with others' individualities and clash with that. We are different people, living together. It's like a bouquet of flowers—see how many different flowers are there.

If it is just one type of flower, it might look a little monotonous. A bouquet should have a variety of flowers. Only then does it looks pretty. All the flowers should stay put in one vase. If this one says, "No, no, no, no, I don't want to be by your side," and if another flower says, "Oh, you are different, I don't want to be next to you," you cannot have a bouquet. An orchard has different fruits, but they all have a common purpose.

The quality that you should develop first is dedication. Dedicate your life for a cause, for the welfare of the humanity, which starts here. Of course, when you think of the welfare of others, automatically you are included in that. It's a double process. You are growing, and you help others to grow.

That is the purpose with which Yogaville is growing. One of the main aims in Yogaville is to lead a dedicated life. The foundation of Yogaville is that. Dedicate yourself completely at the altar of Yogaville.

Anything and everything that could make Yogaville a success should be done by you. Brush aside any pettiness. Know that you are here living for Yogaville. Think that way. Give yourself completely to that.

Every one of you should question, "What should I do to make this a success?" Yogaville will do nothing for you unless you put yourself one hundred percent in the hands of Yogaville. Live for that sake.

Look at some of the Karma Yogis, how beautiful, how happily they are working. I see that when I walk around. You can always see who are all the people who are really doing it for the joy of doing; the joy is there in their faces. How many people do things as a burden or in a half-hearted way? You can't hide it. It's clearly seen.

Do your part, whatever you can; but do it with joy. Anything that you do, you should do with all joy. We all play our parts. If you enjoy it, you can serve more. All should think that way. That way you can make this place really a heaven on earth. The people who come here should feel a heavenly atmosphere here. Let God's presence be felt by the people who visit here.

We see that dedication especially in the examples of the *sannyasis* and ministers. More or less, the organization survives and grows mainly by these two categories, the ministers and *sannyasis*. Ministers are propagators of Integral Yoga very similar to the *sannyasis*. And, it is the service of the *sannyasis* and ministers that encourages the other devotees to come forward and to contribute their energy for the growth.

The other contributors, the lay disciples, have their own work, businesses, jobs, everything; they might not have much time to think of the organization. They come forward to do whatever they can. To inspire them and to make them feel it's a worthy cause to offer something—that is in the hands of the *sannyasis* and ministers.

The swamis wear the orange color, and the ministers wear their robes to show that they are dedicated people ready to serve you. It is a badge. When you see a swami you know that he or she is a public servant. Selfless service is the motto of the swamis and ministers. You can ask them for any kind of help. If they can help you, they will do it. To show the world they are dedicated people you have to have some sign. Each community has a different type of dress to show that.

The significance of the swami's orange color symbolizes that they have burned out all their desires. They have burned out everything that they once called "theirs." In a sacrificial fire, they symbolically throw whatever they call "theirs." They say, "I throw it into the sacrificial fire. I offer it to God." And then, after the service, these things are taken back from the fire and given to them: their dress, their body, their intelligence, their ego—everything has been fired and then given back to them, purified by the fire.

With the pure instruments, they can function without any attachment. So, whatever you put in the fire and take out gets this orange color as a symbol. If they still show some ego, I did not do a good job. I have to re-roast it; because, once you roast the seed, then it won't grow anymore.

By their example, by their service, the other people should feel that, "Yes, this is a beautiful place; it needs growth, and it needs all our help." If others don't come forward to help, it is due to the lack of our example, our lifestyle. We should inspire other members and the public by our example. In that way, the future of the Ashram, Yogaville, and the Integral Yoga organization in general will be taken care of.

John F. Kennedy said, "Ask not what your country can do for you. Instead, ask what you can do for your country." Every one of you should ask, "What should I do to make this a success?" Don't say,

"What can Yogaville do for me?" Yogaville will do nothing for you unless you one hundred percent put yourself in the hands of Yogaville. And that's what makes the difference between ordinary work and work in an ashram like this. We are doing for the sake of everybody.

Once you learn to love this group, then it is easy for you to expand it wider and wider. Ultimately, you expand to include the whole country and the whole world. We see many communities, many religious groups like that: "I love my group, that's all." That is limited love. Sometimes, we come with that purpose, we just stop here and that's it. If you say, "I love Yogaville and not Buckingham," there's no universality in that. That is not our purpose.

We come here to get rooted in that unlimited love. Grow like a banyan tree. A banyan tree loves the first root. And then, gradually, what happens? It branches off and it has roots all over, tap roots. Ultimately, even the central root is gone. It survives with all other roots. Somewhere in Andhra Pradesh in India they found a several thousand year-old banyan tree, the largest and the oldest banyan tree. They still can't find where the original tree started. The original root is gone. And that is the way it should be with us.

In a way that is what we are trying even in Yogaville. It is our village, it is our job. I am just doing my part, you are doing your part. Everybody is needed. No one and nothing is superior or inferior. It is all ours. That kind of feeling of "ours" is what we are trying to develop in a small place. And it should not stop just within this area alone. Then you expand. This is a place where you can grow that feeling of togetherness, loving the entire group.

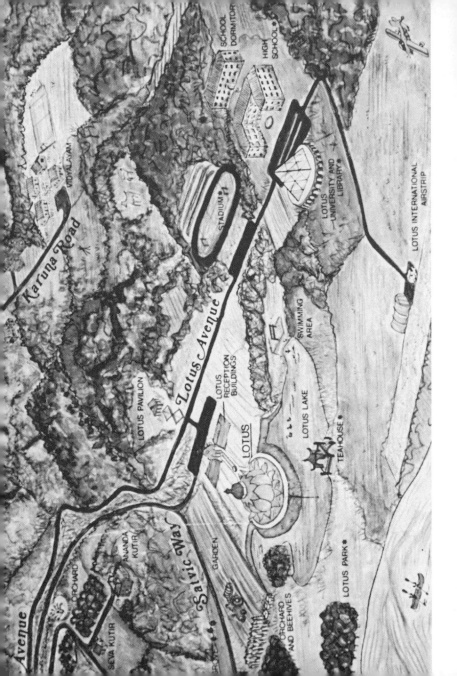

Real love is universal, no matter who she is, who he is, or what it is—plants, animals, people, air, fire, water, everything—the entire nature, the entire creation should be loved equally. That is pure love. Let us learn to develop that kind of unlimited love. Love should expand, expand, expand until it reaches the entire creation. I say the creation, not only the globe. Even the sun, moon, stars, everything is ours. We are part of this galaxy and many, many more galaxies.

The first lesson to be learned from Yoga is to lead a dedicated life. Love expresses itself as dedication and service. The most important thing you can do is to dedicate your life in service. Serve all with your heart and soul, with your life. Serve with your body, mind, and with everything that you possess. Serve the whole universe. Every minute you should remember that you are here to serve others.

If you are dedicated in life, you have eternal joy and peace. If service becomes your motto in life, you will always be peaceful and joyful. What more do you need in life? We do everything to find a little peace, find a little joy; but if we do it with the wrong attitude, we don't find real joy.

Real joy comes by leading a dedicated life. That is what we see in nature. The entire nature exists to serve others. We don't need teachings for all the other species in life because they already live to serve others. So let your motto be, "I am living to serve others. I am living to serve." Everything that you possess was given to you as a gift to be used in service, not to be used for yourself.

The most important thing in life is service, service, service. Keep that in mind. The immediate benefit of that is you are always happy. A person who has dedicated his life or her life to service will never find sadness in life. They always will experience peace and joy.

Trees and flowers don't exist for themselves. Only human beings seem to exist for themselves. That is why Yoga is only necessary for the human beings. That is the reason why people come to ashrams like this—to do everything for others' sake. You think of others and do whatever you can for others. Don't put yourself first. Put God and God's creation first. That is why it is a public place. Nobody owns it. Whatever we do, we do for others' sake. That is what makes an ashram an ashram, Yogaville a real Yogaville.

Offer everything that you can. Accept whatever comes to you. If more people begin to taste that, it will be a beautiful heaven. Even with a limited dedication, you are being recognized as one of the most beautiful communities. Imagine if all of you totally dedicate your lives with no reservations whatsoever.

If you serve well, if you are useful to other people, we always will take care of you. You don't have to worry about yourself. Others should come and say, "Stop that; enough work; go and rest." Others should tell you, "You should eat. You should go and rest. Enough for today."

Try it for some time and see how happy you feel. We should not work for ourselves. "What can I gain? What can I get?" No. Forget yourself and think of others always. That is what makes selfless service, Karma Yoga. When people are really Karma Yogis, that place is a heaven. Wherever selfishness comes, it becomes a hell. So let us learn to be totally, totally selfless and service-oriented—searching for opportunities to serve others. That will make the place a heaven.

Well, words can never bring the real joy. I may talk the whole day about how tasty the sweets are; but, unless you take time to eat, they are just words. Think: "What more could I do to serve?" Let this be a good opportunity for us to renew that dedication and to reevaluate our individual selves. "How much am I doing? How much more can I give? How reluctant am I in giving? How could I improve? What more should I do?"

Yogaville should be a place where there is no, "I, me, mine." You are simply absorbed in the whole. You are part of the whole. Simply go, sleep, think of that goal every day; and all the necessary things to fulfill that goal will come to you automatically. You don't even have to go and ask; because we have picked up a goal that is dear to God. It is the business of God to take care of that. You don't even have to tell God, "I have a goal. Please fulfill it." Instead say, "You put that goal in my mind; it is Your business to fulfill it. I am ready to do my part." You help by putting this goal forward.

By living and dreaming and do doing everything in that name, Yogaville will naturally manifest. God will send all the necessary things: money, people, facilities, opportunities.

Money will come, buildings will come. I don't worry about money. Money should come and beg you, "Come on, come on. I am here. Take it; make use of it." Yes. It should beg you; you shouldn't beg for it. I believe in that. If your goal is great and if your dedication is great, every facility will come to you. Don't think of the dollar. It will come after you. Put the goal forward, march forward. All the rest will be added unto you.

If you become a good Yogi, you will be successful spiritually, socially, materially—in every way. It's really a promise given to us all by no less than the great Lord Krishna himself in the *Bhagavad Gita*. If you see the last *sloka* of the *Bhagavad Gita*, this is what Lord Krishna promises: "Wherever there is Yoga, wherever there is Arjuna and Krishna, wherever the remembrance of the teaching of Yoga from Krishna to Arjuna, there is health, wealth, happiness, joy, success, prosperity, and everything."

Yoga brings us everything. If you lead a pure, yogic life, you don't need to go in search of success, it comes to you. You don't need to look for anything. Everything looks for you. All you have to do is to be a good Yogi. It is almost the same promise given in the Bible. Almost all the scriptures say the same thing: "Seek ye the Kingdom of God first." Let that be your job, your duty. That is all you have to do. You don't have to go seeking one by one—a little vitamin, a little nutritious food, a little brown rice, a little potato, a few dollars.

You don't have to go in search of every little thing. They are all trifling things. Just go after God. Go for it. And where? Within. The Kingdom is within. Seek that first. Then, whether you want it or not, everything else will simply be added into your life. You may not even want them; but they will be there at your feet begging you to take them, to use them, to handle them.

If you become a true renunciate, a truly dedicated Yogi, the scriptures proclaim that the Goddess of Wisdom and the Goddess of Wealth—Saraswati and Lakshmi—will be sitting at your feet on either side, massaging your feet and waiting for your call, your command. You simply say, "Lakshmi, I want a million dollars." There it is. "Saraswati, I want a good answer for this question." There it is. There are many, many sayings like that. These are the promises the scriptures give. "Know *That* by knowing which you will know everything else."

I would like every one of you who live at the Ashram here to feel me in everything. Even when you pick up a pebble, that is me. When you wash a dish, that is me. When you go to your room, that is me—my room, my stone, or me, myself. If you feel that way, then you are never far away from me. You are very close. And that is the truth.

At least Yogaville is my body. Taking care of Yogaville is taking care of my body. And that is what Bhagavan Sri Krishna meant in the *Bhagavad Gita*: "*Manmanaa bhava madbhakto madyaajee maam namaskuru.* If you want to be a good devotee of Mine, think of Me always. Do everything in My name. Offer everything to Me. Surrender to Me completely." That means in everything, everywhere see me. Whatever you do, think of me. Don't think of yourself. Put aside your individual little self. Then, you are never far from God.

Chapter 6–Continue, Continue, Continue!

Friends, it is really beyond my wildest dreams that all these things are happening here in Yogaville. I used to often wonder if all these efforts were worthwhile. But, today, it has been well proven without any doubt that every little effort that we all make is worthwhile.

My message is to keep up the good work. You have come here to Yogaville and you are doing good work. Everybody who comes here appreciates that, and you are making the place, itself, filled with that vibration of peace, health and happiness. All I could say is continue! Keep it up! It is for your happiness. Then I can say, "Ahh, these are my children. This is my Yogaville. This is what I wanted. Here it is, we have achieved it."

I know how capable our people are. Yogaville people are gems. Gems are here. They may not come here as gems. But, the pressure here makes them gems. Carbon goes to the ground and, by the pressure, it becomes a diamond, right? If they want they can create anything here. Yes; that is the proof of what a clear mind can achieve.

Every one of you should feel blessed to be here in this environment. To make it grow we all have to have that total, total dedication. All should be working in unison. No conflicts. It is not easy. Conflicts may come; but, with an open heart, settle it before you go to bed. Don't carry it for a second day. Everybody should remember to help the other people. Even if one person is lagging behind, the commitment is that others should help. It is not one person's work. It is a collective work. We have come together. We have to work together.

How would I rate the Ashram's progress? There is still room to grow, but you are growing. Don't be in a hurry. Grow slowly but steadily. Think in terms of the Ashram. What can I do to make it grow? What can I do to serve people? The Ashram gets a lot of guests. Your aim should be: "How can I serve them?" You are here to serve people. If everybody thinks that way, it will grow faster. It will grow faster because it is all God's property. We are just doing our part of service.

You are progressing well. You are making some mistakes, but you are learning from those mistakes. There is no harm in making mistakes. We all have to make mistakes to learn the lessons. It is growing, growing in the right direction. Many of us forget from day to day what our aim and purpose is. You cannot depend on me constantly to remind you of that. How long will I be here to remind you? I am patient enough to tell you the same thing again and again. There is nothing new I am saying. But even that will come to an end. By the time that comes to an end, it should be registered in your heart.

Life, itself, should be a game. Relax. Enjoy it. When you are relaxed, you can do more service and a better job. You will never even get tired of it. Some people do their jobs sitting in the office, typing or doing some other work. When they go for a vacation on the weekend, they do a lot of physical work and activities. Still it is work, but they enjoy it. They call it a vacation.

Why? If you enjoy it, you can do more work. That way you can make this place really a heaven on earth. The people who come here should feel the atmosphere—a heavenly atmosphere here.

Everyone has a duty to make that happen. All should think that way. Do your part, whatever you can, but do it with joy. Anything that you do, you should do with all joy. You are doing it for the joy of doing it. Play, play. There is nothing serious. You are playing your part.

Yogaville is not just buildings and roads and other things. The people who come from outside see the beauty. They see you. I get so many letters, calls, appreciating the service that they receive here, the care that they receive here. Every guest simply praises you all. Certainly, it is not a surprise to me. And that is Yoga.

We are trying to present our aim to the world, to show how the world should be. We may not be able to achieve this in the whole world; but, if you all put your heart and soul into it, it is possible to achieve it here in Yogaville. And you are achieving that already.

You may not even know it, you may not even realize how important every one of you is here. I always hear glowing tributes from the people who come here just temporarily. Everybody is appreciating what you have achieved here. Don't let it slip down.

All should welcome suggestions to make it better. We are all doing for the common good. Everybody should always remember that. The people are growing and others are noticing it. That really makes me so happy. When you grow like that, and when you fill the place with that kind of beautiful vibration, whoever walks in will immediately feel that. They are bathed in that. And they, themselves, get healed.

Yogaville is a village of health. This whole Ashram, Yogaville, we want to call it a wellness center. We want the place and the people to be well; the children should be well, grownups well—physically, mentally, intellectually, spiritually, socially. The essence of all these philosophies is nothing but, "Be well and do well." Or, as my Master, Swami Sivanandaji, always used to say, "Be good, do good."

There is nothing but health and happiness here. We are trying to charge this place with that. Universal love. That is what we need. With that, any problem can be solved. We have come from all the corners of the globe, a beautiful bunch of people. So, in a way, the whole world is here. If we succeed in making this place a beautiful, peaceful, happy, healthy group, then your mere living here and praying will help the rest of the world. Send all your good thoughts to all those people who need your prayers.

In so many other countries there are a lot of calamities, troubles going on, international rivalry, communal rivalry, poverty, sickness. All those people can be helped by your sincere prayers with a pure heart. So, pray for all. That is why, daily, we repeat the prayer: "*Sarveshaam swasthir bhavatu.*" (May peace be unto all.) It includes all the created species, visible and invisible. When you say "*sarveshaam*" think of that—may the whole universe find peace.

Every day, when you say that prayer, you should think of the meaning and really mean that. Prayers are not just to verbally repeat. Even if you don't repeat it, it should come from the heart. Think of it. That way, even though you may not go out to other countries, praying for others is a great service. And the prayers should come from a pure heart. That is why we are preparing ourselves to be pure so that we can pray for everybody.

But remember charity begins at home. You get well first and your wellness vibration should simply go and influence others. As an unwell person walks near you, they will say, "Hey, I feel comfortable now. I feel all right." Even without your doing anything, you should emit that vibration. That is why, "Physician, heal thyself." You get well and then share that wellness with others.

Already there are many cases of people telling me that their problems vanished. They came here with this problem, that problem, mental problem, physical problem, marital problem, many problems. They just come here and, without even telling anybody their problem, within two to three days it's all gone, miraculously.

I think Yogaville people should be proud to hear what people say. Many say that the moment you walk into Yogaville you feel something very different. The entire Yogaville area is permeated with some special vibrations. I'm just telling you so you will be happy in hearing it; because you were the people who did that. Earlier, there were only rocks and trees. You came; and your thoughts, your actions made the whole place so beautiful.

Every one of you is an important factor for that power. Let us show the world that we can create a heaven right here. We are creating it. Keep up that good work; let it continue. People normally just live, eat, sleep, make money, enjoy life and go away. Nobody will know about them.

As Thiruvalluvar says, "Let the people recognize your life in this world." If not, what is the use? Whether you are born or not who worries about it? Many people come and go, nobody knows.

We come here to contribute something—something beautiful, something great to the world. And Yogaville is a great contribution to the world. Maybe, when you live here you may not even see it that much. But, when others come, they see it. Let that be our contribution so that even the future generations will remember all your great efforts, all your contributions to the world. That way, you become immortal. That way, we fulfill our mission in life. I wish you all that strength and continued guidance to live up to that.

Yogaville is really becoming a heaven on earth. I really thank you and ask you to please make it a beautiful, beautiful center for healing. Let that grow more and more and more. This is our great contribution to the world. In the language of Findhorn, it is going to be the greatest "power point." I wish you good luck and success in bringing that wellness to all those people who approach you.

Become great Yogis, great sages and saints. Excel me. Multiply all the nice qualities. Then I will love you a lot. That is the way you can have perfect love for me. I don't need anything else. All I need is to have the joy of seeing everybody moving around as the real example of genuine Yogis—hail and healthy. Always serene, peaceful, harmonious, no complaints whatsoever. That way you can love me perfectly. What else would a father need? The saint, Thiruvalluvar, says, "The responsibility of a child to the father is to let people admire the child and say, 'Boy, what a meritorious life the father would have lived to have a child like this.'"

People will admire you when they see you there walking like beautiful well-lit, yogic lights, yogic torches: "Look at that. See the way they walk. See the faces glowing. I have never seen them grumbling over anything. How peaceful, how joyful they are, how serviceful they are. I think that man must have done a good job on them." If people say such things, that will make me immensely happy.

If not, I'm not going to be unhappy. I will tell you that also. I'll be still happy. I will say, "I have done my job, that is all." But, certainly, when I see that you are taking that lesson and getting the benefit and making your life beautiful, that will make me even more happy. And, as I said, it happens. You are already doing it. I hear so many comments about Yogaville and Yogavillians. How peaceful they are, how beautiful they are. When I hear that, I feel so happy, satisfied. So keep that spirit.

Yogaville is an example. I am very proud. I am very proud of it. When the time comes to say goodbye to you, I'll be happy saying goodbye to you, because I know you are all wonderful people. The world will be in good hands. We all built Yogaville. When my time comes, I say goodbye. Afterward, it is up to you. You keep it as Yogaville or make it into a rogaville. Tomorrow anything can happen, it is up to you.

I don't know what more to say. Continue, continue, continue your good work as one mind, one heart, in many bodies. Let the whole world be proud of you all. Those who want to see a better world should be able to come here and see that: a miniature world. So, let us collectively make it possible. Make it a heaven. Let God's presence be felt by the people who visit here. Let people come and see us together, all loving and giving, as one family. There is no mine and thine; it is all ours. Let us see that a lot of such communities, Yogavilles, spread out all over. It can happen. That's my dream. May the Lord bless us to achieve that end.

OM Shanthi, Shanthi, Shanthi.

Yogaville.

Yogaville is an aspiration to express the True Self.

Yogaville is an abode of perfect dedication.

Yogaville is a model world of health and harmony; peace and prosperity.

Yogaville is a spiritual center for study, research and growth.

Yogaville is a community expressing the spiritual unity in diversity through a life of purity and serenity.

Yogaville is an embrace to all nations, cultures and creeds.

Yogaville is an embrace to all nations, cultures and creeds.

Yogaville belongs to all who believe in the precepts and life style of Integral Yoga and affirm to follow it.

Come. Let us walk together, talk together, think together and live together.

With love and best wishes,

Ever yours in Yoga,

Swami Satchidananda

The Yogaville Charter handwritten by Sri Gurudev in 1971

His Holiness Sri Swami Satchidananda

His Holiness Sri Swami Satchidananda (Sri Gurudev) is one of the most revered Yoga masters of our time. Sri Gurudev's teachings and spirit guide us toward a life of peace, both individual and universal, and to religious harmony among all people. Invited to visit the United States in 1966 by artist Peter Max and filmmaker Conrad Rooks, Sri Gurudev was quickly embraced by young Americans looking for lasting peace amid the turbulence of the 1960's.

In 1969, he opened the Woodstock Festival with the words: "The whole world is watching you. The entire world is going to know what the American youth can do for humanity. America is helping everybody in the material field, but the time has come for America to help the whole world with spirituality also." The peaceful atmosphere that prevailed throughout the event was often attributed to Sri Gurudev's blessings and message.

Sri Gurudev was ordained a monk in 1949 by his Master, His Holiness Sri Swami Sivananda Maharaj, founder of the Divine Life Society, Rishikesh, India. From the beginning of his spiritual service, Sri Gurudev was a leader in the interfaith movement. His motto, "Truth is One, Paths are Many," is an integral part of his teachings. For more than fifty years, he sponsored interfaith worship services and conferences. His teachings advocate respecting and honoring all faiths. Sri Gurudev was invited to share his message of peace with such world leaders and dignitaries as former U.S. Presidents Jimmy Carter, George H. W. Bush, and Bill Clinton; His Holiness Pope Paul VI, His Holiness Pope John Paul II, His Holiness the Dalai Lama, and former Secretary-General of the United Nations U Thant.

Sri Gurudev is the founder and spiritual guide for the worldwide Integral Yoga® Institutes. Integral Yoga, as taught by Sri Gurudev, combines various methods of Yoga, including Hatha Yoga, selfless service, meditation, prayer, and a 5,000-year-old philosophy to help one find the peace and joy within. Integral Yoga is the foundation for Dr. Dean Ornish's landmark work in reversing heart disease and Dr. Michael Lerner's noted Commonweal Cancer Help program.

In 1979, Sri Gurudev was inspired to create a permanent place where all people could come to realize their essential oneness. He established Satchidananda Ashram–Yogaville near Charlottesville, Virginia. The community is founded on his teachings, which include the principles of non-violence and universal harmony. A focal point of Yogaville is the Light Of Truth Universal Shrine (LOTUS), dedicated in 1986. This unique interfaith Shrine honors the Spirit that unites all the world religions and celebrates their diversity. People from all faiths and backgrounds, from all over the world, visit there to meditate and pray.

Sri Gurudev served on the advisory boards of the Temple of Understanding, the Interfaith Center of New York, the Center for

International Dialogue, and numerous other world peace and interfaith organizations. Over the years, he received many honors for his public service, including the Albert Schweitzer Humanitarian Award and the Anti-Defamation League Humanitarian Award.

In October 1994, on the occasion of the 125th birth anniversary of Mahatma Gandhi, Sri Gurudev was awarded the highest citation of the Bharatiya Vidya Bhavan. He was named an Honorary Patron, joining other luminaries who received this award including, Dr. S. Radhakrishnan, Mother Teresa, and his Holiness the Dalai Lama. In 1994, he was named "Hindu of the Year" by *Hinduism Today*. In 1996, he was presented with the Juliet Hollister Interfaith Award at the United Nations. In April 2002, he was honored with the prestigious U Thant Peace Award. Previous recipients of this award include Pope John Paul II, Mother Teresa, Archbishop Desmond Tutu, and Nelson Mandela.

Sri Gurudev is the author of many books, including *Integral Yoga Hatha*, *To Know Your Self*, *The Living Gita*, and *The Golden Present*, and is the subject of three biographies: *Apostle of Peace*, *Portrait of a Modern Sage*, and *Boundless Giving*.

Born in South India in 1914, Sri Gurudev took *Mahasamadhi* in 2002.

For more information, please visit: www.swamisatchidananda.org